NUGGETS OF GOLD

Josh:

NUGGETS OF GOLD

for relationships

Enjoy the Book.

Tom

Tom and Bev Thompson

Cover design Bev Thompson, Drayton Valley, Alberta, Canada

Library of Congress Control Number: 2007910371
ISBN: Hardcover 978-1-4363-1440-4
Softcover 978-1-4363-1439-8

A publication of

A ministry of Drayton Valley Word of Life Church
Drayton Valley, Alberta, Canada
Web page: dvwordoflife.com

This book was printed in the United States of America.

To order additional copies of this book, contact:
Xlibris Corporation
1-888-795-4274
www.Xlibris.com
Orders@Xlibris.com
45632

Presented to:

____

On the Occasion of:

____

by:

____

Personal Message:

____

____

____

____

____

____

____

____

Date:

____

Contents

We dedicate this book to
Bev's mom & dad who were
sweethearts for 67 years.
They are a true example
of a God centered,
'livin' for each other marriage.
Thank you mom & dad, for teaching
by example what true love really is
and how it behaves.

Hazel Isobel Hanson

Published in sweet memory of mommy:
Hazel Isabel Hanson who went to be with
her Lord July 13, 2005

Foreword

God called Tom and Bev to help us plant and establish our local church. I have had the privilege of being their pastor for many years, and they have been a very effective part of our ministry team.

The ideas in this book are not just words of possibility, but words taken from experience. Tom and Bev's ministry expresses the wisdom of God with practical application. They lead and mentor many couples through teaching and by example.

This book will both inspire and convict any couple that is willing to take responsibility for their relationship. We use this material in our premarriage training sessions.

This is a great investment for anyone who is committed to building and enjoying a great marriage . . . well done, Tom and Bev

Rev. Gary W. Carter
Founder and senior pastor of Drayton Valley
Word of Life Church and Ministries

For some time now, we have struggled with the question of whether another 'marriage' book would be of real value. Our ideas and heart are so basic and simple that we wondered whether people would even be interested in a book of this nature.

While counselling couples who are struggling in their relationship, we have come to realize that it is the 'little things' and basic concepts that a great many couples need to hear.

Our heart is to share with others those basic principles where the 'rubber meets the road'.

We pray that you will glean some very practical and easy-to-apply insights on how to make your relationship not only good, but hopefully, zing!

Tom & Bev

So many people
have lowered their vision and expectation
for their marriages and are just
'hanging in there', trying to survive.
This is not God's plan for his people.
Jesus said, "I have come
that you might have life more abundantly."

Every born again believer is
called to abundant living—
that includes your marriage which is
to be an example to those around you of the
love relationship between Jesus Christ
and His church. We serve an extreme
God who wants to
extremely bless us in our marriages
and all other parts of our lives.
He does this so that we
can be whole and pour His love out
to those around us who are
wounded and lost.

The greatest gift my parents gave me second only to a godly heritage was growing up watching parents who loved each other. You know that God kind of love—putting each other's needs before their own and treating each other with dignity and respect. I never once saw my parents fight or even raise their voices at each other. (Most people find that very hard to believe!) When hard things came at them, they would stand back to back and fight anything and everything that could harm their relationship or the family. They were a team.

I believe Mom and Dad knew and understood the heart of God when it came to marriage and loving each other!

Bev

Through the years, our relationship
has not been
trouble free by any means;
but because of two things,
we have walked through the hard times.

First, we have built our lives on the
foundation of Jesus Christ and established
our relationship on principles
found in the Word of God.
Secondly, we determined to put
each other's interests ahead of our own
and we have worked hard to make it happen.

Protect your relationship against anything that would try to distract you or take you away from it. When you make it your first priority, it builds a soft landing place to come home to at the end of your hectic day.

When you give the very best of yourself to your spouse first and your kids second, you establish a realistic view and understanding in their minds of what love really is—rather than the unrealistic 'in love' understanding they get from TV. This understanding of love in action is something they will take with them into their adult relationships, and it will affect every area of their lives and their future.

Here is a nugget that will save you a great deal of pain and heartache if you apply it. Keep in mind that you can only change you. Don't try to change your spouse, especially by pointing out what is wrong with them! Your constructive suggestions will be perceived as criticisms and will cause them to shut down their hearts to you. Once your spouse doesn't feel their heart is safe with you, it takes a great deal of hard work and time to rebuild the trust you need to have a happy and successful relationship.

God calls His people to excellence. Marriage is one of those areas where it is needed. Don't live your relationship in mediocrity, or you could lose it.

Choose to trust your hearts to each other. You did not marry your spouse so that you could make their life miserable. Keep that thought in your heart and mind when things get rough. Choose to trust your spouse's good intentions.

So much of the success of your relationship comes down to choices you make in your heart, in that quiet place that people don't see—only God does. Don't let circumstances and the chaos of everyday living determine what kind of a marriage you will have. Choose every day to love, appreciate, and honour your spouse.

Never withhold your acceptance or support from each other. There are enough things outside your home that will tear you down without having to face the same thing at home. Do everything in your power to make your home a safe place for the entire family.

The greatest battle in any marriage will be the battle within yourself. Allow God to keep your heart soft and pliable and always be growing and learning to be more like Jesus.

<u>Never pout!!</u> That is the lowest, most immature method of communication that there is.
Not only is it juvenile behaviour that shows a great lack in maturity, but it also establishes a very negative communication pattern in your relationship.

Do you know the things your spouse truly values, what he/she feels passionate about? Set yourself to learn what they are.

The ultimate goal of a loving relationship is
found in 1 Corinthians chapter 13 verses 4 through 8.
Tom and Bev's translation—
Love endures; it hangs on when things look hopeless
It is patient and kind even when the other one is not
Love is not envious or jealous of the other
It does not boast or brag, exulting
itself above the other
It does not act or think arrogantly
It does not act in a way that would
hurt the other and it
does not demand its own way.
Love is not touchy, prickly or resentful
towards the other
It does not keep a record of wrongs or
perceived wrongs, but is happy
when something good happens to the other
even if it has not happened to them
Love chooses every day to believe the
best of the other
It chooses to hold up under the pressures
of daily living as well as in
times of great stress and pain.
It is always ready to believe the best—no matter
what circumstance it faces
It chooses not to fade or weaken or die
Love never becomes obsolete and true love
never comes to an end.

Love is a daily choice not an emotion or feeling.
Love is Action!

When faults in your spouse drive you nuts, look in the mirror—chances are those faults will usually be glaring back at you in one form or another.

Proverbs 16 verse 24 tells us that pleasant, kind, and gentle words bring sweetness to your soul and health to your physical body. Your words are very powerful!

It is almost impossible to stay crabby or disgruntled when you hear children's laughter. It should also be impossible to speak destructive words to someone if you truly love them.

Choose your battles wisely.
Don't get into something just because you have had a bad day and you are irritable or stressed.

Children learn by watching. What they
consider to be normal behaviour will
be what they see in you.
They will treat their spouse and children in the
way they have learned from you.
What heritage do you
want to pass on to your children
and grandchildren?

Deal with negative feelings.
Look at yourself rather than laying blame elsewhere. When you blame others, you will never deal with the issues that the Lord is trying to get you to face.

Remember, when your feelings do not line up with what you know they should be, it is not the feelings that are wrong, but allowing them to dictate your responses that are wrong. Choose to respond in a way that will bring sweetness into your relationship rather than pain.

The first wedding to take place in the history of mankind was officiated by God the Father. One man, one woman, and the blessing of God. What the Lord God was doing that day was far more than just performing a ceremony. He was in fact, establishing the pattern for all marriages to follow for the rest of human history. God did not establish a plan B if they had problems or issues.

To be able to truly love, as God intended us to, we must first know that we are loved. In Romans 5:6-8, we are taught that God loved us so much, that while we still hated and despised Him, He chose to love us and die for us. <u>That is love!</u>

How willing are you to even lay aside some of your plans and desires, your wants, to bless and uplift your spouse?

Sometimes you are better heard
when you don't say a word.

Schedule 'sweet time' with your spouse; make sure there are no distractions. Get Grandma to baby-sit the kids and do something just for the two of you. Go for a walk (hand in hand of course), watch a good movie (snuggle on the sofa and eat popcorn—who knows where it will lead!) Just use your imagination and enjoy each other's company.

Men and women—
are a bit like a train track—each of us is one of the rails. They run parallel, never overlapping but incomplete alone. Just like a train track needs ties to bind it together, we also need to find the 'ties' that bind us to each other. If you do, you will become an unbeatable pair that can handle any pressure or pain that life will throw your way.

Consider this awesome life lesson that we can learn from looking at God's creation. The ears were not built to be closed but our mouth was! When strife raises its ugly head, you can silence it by simply remaining silent and allowing the other person to speak what is on their minds. (This is not the 'silent treatment,' but allowing expression and not having to defend 'me'.)

Get a sense of humour!

Proverbs 17:27-28 tell us that the person who has knowledge, wisdom, and understanding also has a calm spirit. People think a fool is wise when they use their words carefully and sparingly, knowing when to keep their mouth closed. Sometimes it is best just to keep our mouth closed and stay on our knees!

Don't give up!
When things are difficult
and you don't know if you
can hang in there,
hang on a little longer and
remember the little train
in the children's story that
kept going by saying,
"I think I can, I think I can."

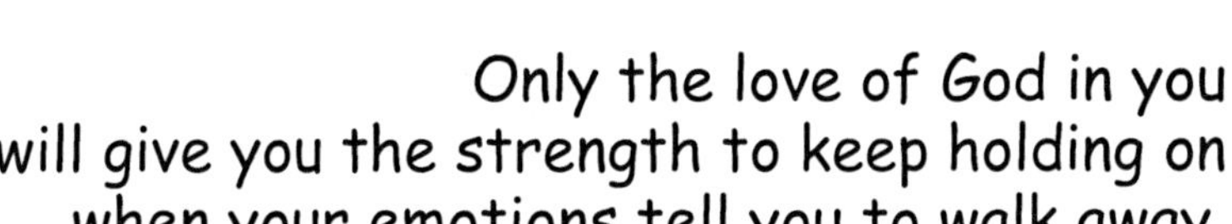

Only the love of God in you
will give you the strength to keep holding on
when your emotions tell you to walk away.

Philippians 4:8 reminds us
to focus our thoughts on what is factual,
accurate, honourable, worthy of our time
and consideration, admirable and true.
We are to think about things that are
pure and lovely, positive and uplifting.
You cannot help but love and appreciate your
spouse when you look at them in the light of
this scripture verse.
Focus on all the things that are right rather than
everything that you feel is wrong.

Keeping a sense of humour goes a long way in keeping love alive! When was the last time you and your sweetheart had a real good 'belly laugh' together? Proverbs 17:22 tells us that laughter is good for the soul—good like medicine when you are ill. Does your relationship need a good shot of laughter? Try applying this powerful principle to your relationship and watch the changes begin to happen.

Never underestimate the power your words can have on your spouse: for good or for evil.

Always be ready to laugh at yourself rather than at others. If you can learn to laugh at yourself and find humour in your humanness, you will be guaranteed a lifetime of fun. You will never run out of reasons to laugh!

Dr. Gary Chapman teaches about the 'love bank'. You can only withdraw what you have already put in. Are you investing into your relationship as much as you expect to get out of it?

If you want to know what fills your heart and mind, listen to your mouth.
How do you speak to your spouse?
Are the words kind and considerate?
Is your tone gentle, kind, or harsh
and condescending?

Deal with negative feelings quickly
so they cannot get a foothold in your marriage
and build walls between you.

Do you consider yourself to be a mature person of godly character? Your words and actions will reveal the truth!

What you value and truly care about
you will pour time and effort into.
How valuable is your marriage to you?

Matthew 22:37 tells us to love the Lord with all our heart, our soul and mind. If we follow this principle in life, the love we have for God will overflow into our relationship with our spouse.

As you follow the example of love set out in 1 Corinthians 13:4-8, the love you have for each other will continue to grow and bloom in ways you will find unbelievable and almost miraculous. In years to come you will look back and marvel at the wonder of the love of God and what He has done in you and the relationship you have with your spouse.

Honour each other!
Show respect to and for each other.
Never overlook your spouse or talk down to them.
Romans 12:10 says to be devoted to one another, honouring your spouse more than yourself.

If you want a good marriage, be a forgiver!

Loving means giving—of yourself!

Do you still have a copy of your original marriage vows? How about pulling them out once a year and renewing them! If you don't have the originals, write new ones, then make a habit of reminding yourself on a yearly basis what you promised each other before God.

Consider Ecclesiastes 4:9-10.
The two of you can accomplish so much more than one of you alone can.
If one of you is weak and falls, the other who is strong at the time, can reach down and pull the weak one up.
Keep in mind that the next time the situation could be reversed, and the one who is weak this time could be the strong one.
Utilize each other's strengths.

The devil loves it when we point fingers and find fault in our spouse rather than dealing with the faults and issues in ourselves. Always keep your heart and mind open to the attitude of 'Lord change me.'

Oneness and sameness are two totally different things. Accept your differences, and don't try to make your spouse like you.

Successful couples know that you cannot have a great marriage without work; it takes deliberate decisions and steps to get where you want to go. Establish the steps you need to take and begin the journey towards an absolutely awesome marriage. Start today!

Do you know your purpose and destiny, why God placed you here in this season of time?
What is your vision for life as an individual and as a couple?
Ask the Lord to show you what He wants you to do, then write it down. Keep it someplace where it is visible and hard to miss.
It will give you a focus point to hang onto when you are going through tough times.

See the importance of who your spouse is rather than what he or she can do for you.

Find a 'signal' that you can give each other when a disagreement is heating up into a war.
Have a 'time out' of ten to fifteen minutes, where each of you can get away and focus on looking at things from a different perspective.
Make a point of trying to see things from your spouse's point of view.

Make it a goal in your life to walk in kindness and love no matter what the circumstances. Remember you get out of something what you put into it.

Keep an attitude of forgiveness in the forefront of your relationship.

When conflict arises and you are trying to deal with it, keep eye contact and hold hands—stay connected emotionally and physically. It is very hard to fight dirty when keeping eye contact and holding hands (lovingly!).

If you allow negative thought patterns to be a part of your thinking, it is really hard (almost impossible) to see and think the best of your spouse or anything else for that matter!

A bitter and resentful spirit is to a marriage;
what toxic waste is to the earth.
It will eventually suffocate
and destroy it!

Galatians 6:9 tells us not to lose heart or give up when doing the right thing because in God's perfect timing and when you have reached a place of maturity, you will receive what you have worked so hard for.
If things are not the way you would like them to be today, just keep on working at it and doing what is right.
It will pay off someday!
Do not lose your courage or give up hope!

Unless both of you work at
keeping your relationship intimate and kind,
you will eventually find yourselves
moving in opposite directions.

Deal with each other in mercy as God deals with you rather than in harshness and judgment. Be as loving and gentle to your spouse as you want God and your spouse to be to you.

Every morning when your feet hit the floor, you have the choice of what attitude you will walk in today. Dr. Robert H. Schuller says to put on a positive attitude like you put on a piece of clothing. If it helps, act it out.
Pick your positive attitude up off the top of your dresser and put it on like a shirt. You will be amazed at how it helps you start your day right and stay right!

We cannot rewrite the past; however, we can write our future by the choices and decisions we make today.

Learn to be flexible. Issues of life do not fit into perfect little boxes. There will be times when you just have to be willing to bend a little!

Deal with hurts and misunderstandings immediately, or they will begin to drive a wedge between you.

Here is a tongue in cheek: A preacher once jokingly said, "Don't go looking for the perfect mate, just take anyone, they'll be a different person in six month from now anyway!" Give your spouse a reason to be glad they chose you!

There will be times when your spouse points out areas in your life that need improvement. Instead of becoming offended, quietly mention that they may have a point and you will consider what has been said. Think about it! Take a good honest look at yourself you may be surprised by what you learn.

Remember, what goes around comes around.
Nowhere is this truer than
in a marriage!

If you have a fight and agree to bury the hatchet, make sure you bury the entire thing including the handle! (Oh, and not in your spouse's skull either!)

Be kind
even when your spouse isn't!

One way to build an excellent relationship is to imitate one. Find someone's marriage you would like yours to be like and hang out with them. Ask lots of questions. Anyone who has a good relationship loves to see others have one too. Most happily married couples are more than willing to share their wisdom and experience.

Love is strangled when we allow ourselves to focus on things we don't like in our spouse, but blooms when we focus on the things we do.

Money can often be a source of conflict in marriages. Manage it as though it belongs to the Lord, and remember it does! You are just a steward of it.

Appreciate each other's differences rather than resenting them. Consider the old saying, "If you were the same, one of you wouldn't be necessary."

Be a peacemaker!
This does not mean you avoid conflict. Rather, make every effort to bring about a peaceful resolution in all circumstances where there could be conflict. Make peace a priority!

Sometimes you need conflict to bring issues in your relationship to the surface so you can face them and deal with them productively.

As a spouse, make your marriage relationship top priority over all others. Never sacrifice your marriage relationship for kids, friends, work, parents, sports . . . etc.

Every problem that comes up is a potential opportunity to learn and grow. Choose to respond positively to whatever is happening to you. You decide the outcome by your choices. Every marriage has its hard times, so the choices you make today will decide the future of your marriage and how good it will be.

People are precious—hold them close to your heart and material things loosely!

When in a disagreement, spend less time defending your position and more time taking charge of doing what is right for the two of you combined.

Never complain to others about your spouse! If you need to talk about problems, talk about them on your knees to your Heavenly Father. Thank Him for your spouse and the good things He is working in you through him/her. If you need help and godly advice, see your pastor, a Christian marriage counsellor or someone who will give you the tools you need to make your relationship successful.

Want to feel good about yourself? Pour your very best into your spouse and relationship; let everything and everyone else get second best.

There will be times in your relationship when you have to live by the principles in the Word of God (when emotions are running you ragged and you are not feeling so 'loving'). Love is not an emotion, a 'warm fuzzy' as the movies portray, but a decision, a choice you make.

How do you begin your day? Positively or negatively?
How do you greet your spouse
first thing in the morning?
If your first response is not positive,
Dr. Robert H. Schuller suggests you hold your tongue until you are thinking clearly enough to be positive. Not only do you set the tone of your day positively, but your spouse's too.

We are all guilty of making excuses for ourselves at one time or another. An excuse will never get you anywhere except around the mountain to the same problem again.
So stand and face the problem.

James 1:5 tells us that if we are short on wisdom in a situation and don't know how to act or don't know what to do,
ask God and He will gladly give you His wisdom.
In fact, it pleases Him to do so!

It takes two to fight.
One person cannot fight alone!
Be on guard against anything
that would set you against each other and
cause you to lose sight of
what God intended marriage to be.
Look for reasons to defend each
other and build each other up.

There is no place for pride in a marriage.
Matthew 5:34-35 remind us of this truth.
If there is an offense between the two of you,
don't wait for the other one to apologize.
You be the one to break the ice. This is incredibly
hard, but well worth it!

DATE! Just because you are married
doesn't mean you should stop dating!
Continue to put your best foot forward and
keep the romance in your marriage.

Because money can often be an issue in marriage, keep this thought in mind.
If you don't have it, don't spend it! Learn to wait for things; anticipation can be half the fun of getting what you want.

Conflict is inevitable.
When you withdraw from a confrontation, basically you are 'turning off' either by pouting, leaving, or giving the 'silent' treatment.
This is an extremely poor way of dealing with issues because they never get dealt with and will always come up again. Set up guidelines for fair fighting when things between you are good so that you won't move into fighting dirty when things get tense between you.

Build each other up!
Look for and find reasons to let
your spouse know you appreciate them.
Let your spouse know you're proud of them and approve of them. Speak with words but also with your actions and body language.

Worry about money before you spend it, not after it is already spent!

Instead of complaining about what your spouse isn't, thank God for what he/she is and focus on those things.

A great intimacy builder—sit down together and share a dream. We used to draw up house plans for our 'dream acreage' we never thought we would ever own, but it didn't matter. We had fun sharing, drawing, laughing together and bouncing ideas off each other.

What happens to you is sometimes beyond your control; however, your response isn't.
Be aware of your responses.

Intimacy can grow and bloom in a relationship where both parties are committed to creating an atmosphere of safety, one where you are able to share your hearts and deepest feelings without fear.

One of the greatest keys to the success of our marriage is found in Ephesians chapter 4 the second part of verse 26—don't let the sun go down on your anger. We made this vow to each other over thirty-five years ago and have always kept it. (We have had a few very, very long nights over the years, but never have we allowed ourselves to go to bed without working through an issue.

Your spouse will never outgrow their need for your affirmation, praise, and honest appreciation.

You are the guardian of your spouse's heart; it is fragile and delicate, so handle it lovingly with care as you would wish your heart to be handled.

A marriage isn't automatically good just because two people are 'in love'. It takes a great deal of hard work! However, work can be a lot of fun if you have the right attitude towards it.

Maturity is the ability to look in the mirror and see the person who is responsible for your actions and reactions. Don't blame your spouse!

SMILE! It takes far fewer muscles to smile than it does to frown. The old saying that it increases your face value has truth to it too! Everyone likes to receive a smile.

Let your strengths compliment and balance your spouse's weaknesses rather than using them as a weapon against the one you are to care for and cherish.

Never get so accustomed to having your spouse around that you take them for granted. There is always someone out there who would love to have what you have!

Proverbs 3:6 tells us that as we acknowledge God, recognizing Him as a vital part of our lives, He will direct our steps and make our paths straight before us.

Seek God individually and as a couple. Allow Him to be the center of your relationship, and He will show you how to walk with each other in a way that pleases him and makes your marriage awesome in the process.

It is more important to bring peace into a situation than it is to win. Consider what you can do to bring a positive resolution to a negative situation, and then do it. Be a peacemaker.

If you want to be whole and complete, and able to meet the needs of your spouse, let God be your 'need' supplier and you will have more than enough to give to your relationship.

The more mature you are, the less you demand 'my way' and the more you are interested in meeting your spouses needs and strengthening your relationship.

If you desire to be loved, be lovable! Work on your attitudes every day.

When things get tough, sit down and write out a list of ten things that attracted you to your spouse in the first place.

Proverbs 12:18 tells us that there will be those who speak carelessly without thinking about how it will affect others, and it will pierce the heart like a dagger leaving deep wounds. There is, however, the truth that the caring words of a wise person can also bring life and healing. Consider your words!

Allow the Holy Spirit in you to bring health and healing in your relationship rather than strife and pain.

When you are facing trials and struggles in your relationship, there is always a way through. Give your negative feelings and thoughts to God (those things that lock you up inside and defeat you) and look for positive things in the Word of God to focus on and replace the negative thought patterns.

Marriage is not a fifty-fifty deal like we have been taught. There is no way that we can figure out if our efforts have taken us halfway. Both of us have to be willing to give 100% and more.

Rather than demanding, how about making your wishes and desires known in a loving, gentle tone? Listen to yourself!

Determine in your hearts to grow with each other and not away from each other. No relationship stands still. You are either moving closer together or apart. At any given time in any relationship, we may feel either appreciated and loved or unappreciated, stressed, overworked, taken for granted, etc. Make the right choices and put out the necessary effort to build unity and oneness in your marriage. Instead of sitting back and waiting for your partner, why not be the first to step toward the other?

When you pour the love of God into your spouse, you are investing in eternity. How lasting are the things you value most? What are you pouring your heart and energy into?

At the same time each year, how about sitting down together and honestly looking over the past year. Write each other a letter, reaffirm your love and affection, make a note of areas you would like to see improve in your life, and how you would like to work at seeing these improvements. Note the areas of improvement and congratulate yourselves. Seal your letter to be opened the same time next year. Choose a date that is significant so you are more inclined to follow through.

Learn to appreciate your spouse's uniqueness. Don't try to change them into another you, but use each other's strengths to build a greater and stronger fortress for life to contend with.

We once heard marriage described like this: Marriage is like a beautifully wrapped but empty gift box. Unless you put more into it than you take out, it will never be anything more than a facade—looking good on the outside but hollow, empty, and painful where it counts.

Married couples that are in love can communicate a thousand love notes with just a glance.

Plan a budget; it helps you keep your finger on your finances.

Treasure the love you are given; it will survive all the storms life can throw your way if you cherish it.

The smallest act of kindness is worth far more than the greatest intentions.

James 1:19-20 tells us to be quick to hear what is being said and slow to speak. Consider this principle from the word of God; next time there is strife or contention trying to come between you and your sweetheart, listen and hear beyond their words to what their heart is saying.

It isn't the 'big' things you do for each other that show you care but the 'little' things that truly say "I value you."

Learn to air out your differences in the 'quiet of the moment'. Set aside a time to discuss issues that could become a problem. It is unproductive to 'discuss' when tempers are hot and emotions are ragged.

Find yourselves a godly couple that have a marriage you would like yours to be like and who have years of a good marriage under their belt. Ask them to mentor you. Become accountable to them and allow them to speak into your relationship and personal life.

Do you want a 'super glue' that will keep your relationship alive and vibrant for years to come? Do fun positive things together that create great memories—those memories that will be talked about long after the glow of youth has worn off. One of my superglue memories is when our first child was born. Tom made a point of coming to the hospital to see me every morning at seven thirty before he went to work. Some of our superglue memories are the times we went camping together as a family, building snow forts with the kids and coaching soccer—what are yours? Start building memories together today that will continue to bring laughter and togetherness for years to come.

Guard the heart of your spouse; it is the most precious gift you will ever be given. Do everything in your power to build companionship and security into your home.

Consider these teachings of Jesus:

Be willing to be last rather than wanting to be first

Be willing to serve rather than expecting others to serve you

Love your spouse with the same depths as you love yourself

Give all of yourself without expecting anything in return

Lay down your life for the other—in other words, place your wants and desires on the bottom shelf and live for your spouse

There will always be conflicts and irritations when two people combine their lives. It is how you deal with those conflicts and irritations that will make or break your love for each other. Choose to be merciful and forgiving even if you feel your spouse does not deserve it. Unless you are perfect, there will be times when you will be in need of mercy and forgiveness, so respond accordingly.

Dr. Norman Wright teaches that marriage is a school where we learn flexibility and living unselfishly. It forces us to grow continually and rethink ideas, reactions, and character. Ask yourself:
am I willing to change and grow?

If you spend time with your sweetheart and create a memory, it will always be with you both. If you are too busy to play and just buy something for them, it will get broken, worn out, and even forgotten.
What are you storing up in the heart of your loved one? This principle is very easily applied to children as well. Consider your time as the most valuable gift you can give them.

No matter where your relationship is at the moment, it can always get better if you are both willing to work at it.

Listening is a needed skill for a great marriage. Gain all the skill you can in this area. Use these skills to truly hear the heart of your spouse. Learn to hear the intent behind the words, not just the words.

Once in awhile do the unexpected; throw your sweetheart for a loop. Do something wild, crazy, and fun—something just for them! (Your sweetheart will love it!)

When you are looking for negatives in a relationship, you are guaranteed to find them. If on the other hand you teach yourself to look for positive things, you will begin to recognize them more and more frequently. Train yourself to look for positives!

Always be loyal to your spouse, defend them before others even if they might be wrong. (Just the way you would want them to stand up for you!) Defend each other's back.

Do you know that you will never totally understand your mate or be able to meet every one of their needs? That is why God has to be your source of self-worth. The more intimate you are with God, the more He will show you how to relate to and understand your spouse.

Make a note to listen—really listen to yourself when you speak to your spouse. There are times when you will have to make adjustments to your tone of voice and expression if you want to be heard.

Get involved in something bigger than yourself; give to others out of who you are. Consider a sponge that fills up but doesn't pour out, it becomes stagnant and stinks; but if it is squeezed, it is able to absorb more. Squeeze yourself, be a giver and watch your heart come alive.

If your marriage is struggling and you need help working through conflict, don't be afraid or too proud to find someone you trust who has the maturity, the experience, and the godliness to give you good advice, and who will be willing to walk through it with you. Make sure the one you choose will not take sides but work with you to see you both win. Keep in mind that next to God, your relationship is the most important thing in the world. Don't let foolish pride or fear keep you from getting help.

Make it a habit of thanking God for your spouse every day.

Always be willing to try new activities with your spouse to encourage 'oneness'. Sometimes it is those little things you do for each other that puts the sparkle and zest into your relationship. Years ago, I took up cycling and he took up horseback riding. Our willingness to step out of our comfort zone for each other in past years helped to establish where we are today in our relationship.

One of the strongest cords a couple can develop to bind their marriage together is to pray with each other. The old saying, "the family that prays together stays together", has a great deal of truth to it.

When your communication breaks down and you find your relationship growing cold, be willing to sit together and quietly discuss your problems. Your willingness to do this is an indication of how committed you are to making your marriage work. Don't let pride get in the way.

If you put in the effort to 'like' your spouse
and work at being likable too,
your relationship will succeed
far beyond your wildest dreams.

Remember, marriage problems can very often arise over money issues.Think of it this way. It isn't necessarily the high cost of living in our society today that gets us into trouble as much as the horrendous cost of living above our means that messes us up. Be willing to plan for and wait for things you want rather than getting into the burden of a debt load.

Lord, grant me the desire and the grace to
accept my love the way he/she is, knowing
that I can't change them; the strength to change
the one I can, and the wisdom to know I'm
the only one I can change.

Once you're married, leave your parents. Make your spouse your home and your security. Concentrate on and give the best of yourself to your relationship. Remember that it is OK to love your folks, but never put them before your spouse.

Unforgiveness in a relationship builds a wall, and justifying your behaviour only fortifies that wall. Knock down a wall today! Let go of any unforgivenss you may have in your heart toward your spouse.

Instead of ignoring or running from problems in your marriage, face them head-on. Ask God to show you a way through them rather than trying to avoid them. Remember that you and your spouse are one. It was God's design to make you one, and it gives him great pleasure when you involve him in your everyday living.

Tell your spouse how important and valuable they are to you! Everyone likes to hear they are special and needed, especially from someone they have given their hearts to!

Be willing to sacrifice 'me' for 'us'. Remember it is what you committed to do when you said "I do."

Meet each other at the door with the big S word (smile!) when one of you has been gone. Throw in a hug too! Let your spouse know that you are glad to see them and they brighten your day when they are there.

Matthew 6:19-20 talks to us about tithes. Tithing to the work of the Lord shows you where your heart is, and then keeps it in the right place. It keeps money from becoming too important and keeps other things that should be important in their place.

Psalms 103:12 tells us that as far as the east is from the west, that is how far God removes our sins and shortcomings from us when we ask for his forgiveness. When God has forgiven us, our sins are as though they never happened in his eyes.
The Lord desires us to live in the same attitude of forgiveness toward other people as he has for us. (That includes our spouse!)

If you want a good marriage, you have to like work because that is what it takes!

People who focus on the past are reactive, always using the past as an excuse for poor behaviour. Those who keep their eyes focused on the future are proactive. Become proactive in your marriage relationship by looking for opportunities to make positive things happen. You do the right thing, and allow God to work on your behalf.

A great man of God, Dr. Robert H. Schuller teaches this concept:
If you really want to live, you have to give of yourself to others. This truly is the key to walking in blessing and prosperity.
Apply this principle to your marriage.
Everything we have is a gift from God.
Be a good trustee of the life of your spouse.
Be generous and be giving, and you will discover a life richer than you ever thought was possible.

Consider this truth taught in Proverbs 21:21.
When you follow righteousness (right standing with God) and mercy, you will find life and honour.
Let me define mercy according to the dictionary—compassion, kindness in excess, a disposition to forgive, gentleness, tenderness, etc.
Walk in mercy with your spouse every day, and you will have a home filled with the peace and love of God.

Jesus pointed out that it is the 'love' of money that is the root of all evil. Don't let money rule or dictate how smoothly your relationship runs. Some of the greatest times of 'oneness' can be when things are tight and you draw together to battle side by side rather than pulling apart and allowing the situation to drive a wedge between you.

What is taking place inside our heart (the work God is doing to change us into better people) is far more important than the circumstances of our life. Allow God to make the changes in you that he needs to make.

Sometimes what makes a marriage above average are the things left unsaid. Consider the effect your words can have on the heart and self-worth of your spouse.

Catch the curve balls even the foul balls that life throws at you. Ask the Lord to show you how to take them and make your relationship stronger because of them, rather than letting them knock you down.

Do you and your spouse have a goal or vision together, something to work together toward? Work together, grow together! Working side by side towards a goal will only draw you closer!

How and what you think determines what you do. Attitude in marriage means everything! Choose what you think on carefully and wisely! It can make or break your relationship.

Just as a woman desires her man to be strong, gentle, and understanding, so a man desires his wife to be warm, tender and loving, and on his side!

Selfishness is the greatest enemy to a marriage that there is. It is vital that a couple learn to live for each other for the good for the relationship.

Learn to become mutually dependant on God and allow that to overflow into a healthy dependence on each other.

United we stand, divided we fall. We have heard this saying but never has it been truer than in marriage. Make your spouse your ally, not your foe.

Have common friends. Put in the effort it takes to build common friends. It is not good that the husband has his circle of friends and the wife has hers. Common friends help to build unity into your marriage.

Proverbs 15:17 tells us that it is better to have a meal of plain veggies with salt and pepper and smothered in love than prime rib where strife and contention are. When it comes down to the bottom line, it really does not matter what you have materially. If there is anger and strife in your home, you really have nothing.

Conflict very often comes from poor communication; what was said was not what was heard. If you are not sure of the intent behind what you heard, just ask your spouse if what you heard is what they were really saying. Even after thirty-five years of marriage, there are times when we don't get what the other is saying; but because we have built a positive and secure relationship, we are able to ask each other "Did you mean . . ." or "What are you trying to say?"

The only time you truly fail in your relationship is when you give up; so try, try, and try again!

Stand united in agreement on issues that are important.

As for me and my house, we will serve the Lord! This attitude will make you a winning combination!

Proverbs 21:23 tells us that the person who guards his mouth and tongue keeps his soul from troubles. This is so true in a marriage! Consider your words and the effect they will have on the one you love before you speak.

Learn to patiently watch and listen. Be careful not to react inappropriately. Many times things are not as they first appear to be.

It is wonderful to adore and appreciate your spouse, but it needs to be verbalized and shown by your actions. Those little loving things you say and do let your sweetheart know they are loved and cherished.

Walk a mile in each other's shoes once in awhile; it will give you a better appreciation and understanding of each other.

Talk is easy—
it is hearing that is the tough part!

Love births and grows love. Hostility and resentment destroy it. Remember you always reap what you sow.

Be more considerate and thoughtful of your spouse than anyone else!

Life can present some hard, trying times; but when you have worked through those trials, make every effort to restore some fun to the relationship. Learn to laugh again.

Only an insecure person will try to 'fix' or change their mate. Allow your spouse the liberty to be himself or herself and appreciate the beauty of who they are.

Don't battle over insignificant things. Choose your battles wisely!

Proverbs 15:1 tells us that soft answers turn away anger, resentment, and insecurity; but a harsh word (even a harsh or condescending tone) can stir them up.

Time—one of the most valuable gifts you can give your spouse and family.
Be generous with it!

Meet with God every day and let him set the tone for your day. When you feel secure and affirmed in your relationship with God, it allows you to be more giving in your relationship with your spouse and those you come in contact with through the day.

Yesterday shaped who you are today, just as today is shaping what you will be tomorrow. So what do you want to be, and where do you want to be tomorrow? Make the right choices that will take you where you want to go.

Proverbs 15:2 tells us that the wise person uses knowledge properly, thinking before they speak. A fool speaks without considering or thinking, they say things that should never be said.
Be aware of what you are speaking!

What do you speak over your spouse when talking to others? Do you stop to consider your words and how they could hurt or build up the one you love?

When you have a difference of opinion or a quarrel, ask yourself this question, "In the light of eternity or even ten days from now, what difference will this make?"

Learn to have fun together, enjoy being 'us'. Determine in yourself to learn to enjoy some of the things your spouse enjoys, then join in and do them with him/her.

When having an argument or quarrel, never bring out the dirty laundry. I'm not talking about dirty socks and underwear here, but about issues that have been pushed down and never dealt with. Stick to the issue at hand so at least that issue can be dealt with.

Proverbs 16:32 teaches us that the person who is slow to get mad is better than one who is very powerful, and the one who controls himself is better than someone who is strong enough to overthrow a government. Take control of your emotions, don't let them control you! Be a better person than the next guy! This is extremely good advice for a marriage.

Anger is usually a secondary emotion. When anger arises in your relationship, stop to analyze what the first emotion is; for example, fear, rejection, offense, hurt, frustration, etc. In the long run, this will save you a great deal of grief.

If you do not deal with issues as they arise,
they will just resurface again and again,
(often under the guise of something else)
until they are dealt with or they tear you apart.

Always be teachable!
None of us have reached the place
where we know it all!

Proverbs 17 and the beginning of verse 17 tells us that a friend loves at all times.
Are you each other's best friend?
The best foundation for a successful marriage second only to loving God is this principle!
Examine your relationship.
If your spouse is not your best friend, then begin today to build a friendship.
Find common interests—
something you can build on—then start building!

Forgiveness is
an act of the will, a choice, not a feeling.
Choose to forgive when the feeling isn't there;
walk it out and the feeling will follow.

Want to be treated well?
Look inside yourself and ask yourself this:
how do I treat my spouse?
Be thoughtful and kind before you expect
to be treated that way.

It is the positive history you have built together through the years that lets you continue to be sweethearts and lovers when the skin sags and the figure is gone. You are still beautiful in each other's eyes because you see beyond the flesh tent to your spouse's real beauty inside.

The love you give away is the only love
you ever really keep. Give your
sweetheart lots of love—
the 1 Corinthians 13:4-8 kind of love!

Attitude is everything!

We don't recall where we heard this story, but it really tells it the way it is!

A woman walked into her pastor's office and announced in a rather belligerent tone of voice that she was divorcing her husband. "Oh you poor dear, he must be very cruel and abusive," her pastor said. "Oh no, not at all!" the woman replied. "Well then, he must be a horrible, cold, unfeeling father," the pastor continued. "Oh my goodness no, he is a marvellous dad; the kids adore him," she replied emphatically. "Well, that only leaves me to conclude one thing," the pastor continued, "he must have had an adulterous affair." "No," she replied in a very subdued tone of voice, "I know he has never cheated on me!" "Wonderful, this is fabulous!" the pastor said. "if you don't want him, give me his phone number because I have at least thirty women in this congregation alone who would give their right arm for a man like that. Why, I can have him out of your hair in no time!"

Origin of this story unknown

She left the office with a totally different perspective of what she had!

What perspective do you use when looking at the one God has given you?

There are no perfect marriages
because there are
no perfect people. NOT EVEN YOU!

Often during a conflict,
we are so tuned into our own hurts that we are
unable to hear what our spouse is trying to say.
Train yourself to hear beyond the words spoken,
deliberately listen for the heart intent behind
what is being said.

Conflict—stepping-stones or stumbling blocks?
It all depends on how you look at it
and how you respond. Choose
to make it work for you not against you.

The old saying "If you can't say something nice
don't say anything at all"
can come in real handy when
applied to a situation of conflict.

Unless you are a 'one in a million' couple, don't hang wallpaper (or do renovations) together! We never paint together either. There are some things you can do together and some that you can't.
Learn what they are. This little tip alone could save you a few rough spots in your relationship!

Differences in background and upbringing can cause tensions in a marriage.
Be willing to sit down and discuss these areas until you can work out a compromise that both of you are happy and comfortable with.

Thoughtless and unkind words can erode and destroy your spouse's self-esteem. Always make every effort to build the esteem of your sweetheart; it's called honour and respect!

Men and women are so different!
Why did God make us this way?
How often do you hear these kinds of questions?
Here is how we look at it.

The Bible tells us that God created man in his own image. When he put Adam to sleep and removed a part of him to create woman, Adam was no longer whole and the complete image of God.
God then brought the woman to Adam, and they became one.
We would like to suggest that a man is no longer complete alone, but it takes his coming together with his wife for either of them to be complete.
It is only as we learn to love each other as God designed us to love, that the true reflection of God's image can be seen by the world around us.

It is far more important to *be* the right person than it is for you to find the right person!

God takes your marriage very seriously—do you?

The expression 24/7 is the perfect description of the equation for building a great marriage.

As couples, it is our responsibility to encourage and build each other up. When was the last time you let your spouse know how much you need and appreciate them?

When you want to share the love of Jesus
with your spouse, use words only if necessary.

Where are you headed?
Set goals and write them down—
three-month goal, six-month goal,
twelve-month goal, five-year goal, etc.
Don't just let life happen to you,
make it happen for you!

Boundaries in marriage are a vital necessity. Establish those 'fence lines', and it will establish a security for both of you. In every relationship there are areas where we 'just don't go'. Learn these areas in your spouse and respect them.

Be quick to hear and accept truth from each other even when it hurts your pride. Nobody knows you as well as your spouse.

The greatest ingredient for a successful marriage is spiritual compatibility. When you are both reading the same owner's manual (the Word of God), you will always have a solid foundation to refer to.

Proverbs 19:11 tells us that wisdom in a person makes them slow to get angry, and they are esteemed and honoured because they can overlook wrongs done to them.
Apply this principle to your marriage relationship. How very wise and mature it is to overlook those little things in each other that can cause irritation.

When communicating, body language can say every bit as much as or more than our words do!

A marriage that is in big trouble does not have to end in divorce. Dr. Robert H. Schuller teaches that we can take our hurts and turn them into something beautiful. Take the painful situation you may be in and set your face firmly toward a positive solution.
Life does not have to stay as it is.

How we choose to focus our minds will affect how we look at life. This is called attitude, and it affects absolutely every area of our lives.

Celebrate each other's uniqueness, and make your marriage the envy of those around you. Let your love and commitment to each other glow! Be irresistible to others. There is no greater compliment in the world than when someone wants their marriage to be like yours.

Today, make a conscious effort to do a kindness for your sweetheart that you have not done before. Go ahead! Step out of your comfort zone.

So much of what we have conflict over is really totally insignificant and not worth the effort to fight over. It takes so much more effort to fight than it does just to live together in peace and companionship.

Never expect or demand from your spouse what you are not first willing to be or do.

Be generous with encouragement and praise, and both of you make the effort to keep blame and criticism out of your marriage.

Forgiveness is the most vital ingredient there is for a happy and successful marriage. Matthew 6:14-15 tell us that if you forgive those who have done something hurtful to you, then your Heavenly Father will forgive you. However, if you refuse to forgive, then your Heavenly Father will not and cannot forgive you. We all want the mercy of our Heavenly Father; therefore, we have to extend mercy and grace to those who hurt us. Because we are people, we will hurt and be hurt by the one we love; so remember, God will deal with us in the same way that we deal with each other.

Don't let yesterday take up too much of your today. We don't want to forget yesterday because that is where we learned the lessons we need for today. We do not, however, want to get stuck in the past either, so let go of the hurts and remember the valuable lessons you learned and apply them to where you are now. Let them make you a better wife or husband.

In any situation, never side with someone else against your spouse. Always stand true, defending their back. This is called LOYALTY!

If you want to be loved, love your spouse with everything in you. Put more effort into your relationship than you do anything else outside the home.

Marriage is tough enough when you have two emotionally healthy people. If you struggle with your self-worth—and many of us do—then seek help.
Find someone you trust like a pastor or a counsellor who will teach you to focus on what God says you are and what he designed you to be. Learn about God's purpose and destiny for your life.

Know your spouse; make every effort to learn what pleases your sweetheart, then do it!

Make every effort to be a pleasant and contented person. It is far more enticing to be married to a pleasant person than to a miserable one!

Remember that there will always be a certain degree of mystery between men and women. This is a good thing, as it keeps your life interesting! After thirty-five years, we can still pleasantly surprise each other at times.

If someone wants to give you advice for your marriage, look at their marriage. Is there something there that you would want in your relationship?

Work at liking each other! Liking each other helps you to overlook little irritations and shortcomings that might otherwise become problem areas.

Build your marriage relationship on the foundation of your relationship with Jesus. The more intimate you are with him, the closer you will move toward true intimacy with each other. (We guarantee it!)

Make the time to discuss ways that you can strengthen your relationship
then focus on one at a time.
When you are both comfortable in that area, choose another one to focus on.
You can be sure your life together will never get boring or dull.

It is only in the atmosphere of acceptance and forgiveness that a marriage is able to truly flourish. It is easy to become offended at each other so always be on guard against it.

Choose forgiveness.

Don't take yourself so seriously!
Nobody else does.

Proverbs 23:7 teaches us about our thoughts. What have you been allowing in your thoughts? Focus on the beautiful things you saw in your spouse when you were first attracted to them. If you need help to refocus on the positive things, make yourself a 'positive' list. Put your list in a place where it will be a visible reminder every day. As you train yourself to focus on the good, other things will come to mind that you can add to the list. After a while, you will see your spouse totally differently than you did before.

Unless you both work at keeping each other as 'my sweetheart', your relationship can very easily move from "sweetheart and lovers" to boring, mundane, and unexciting partner. Don't let this happen! Work at staying in love with each other.

If we as couples would invest as much time in building our marriages as we invest in our favourite pastimes (like watching TV, sports, shopping, work, 'me'), there would be far fewer divorces and a great many more happy and peaceful homes.
Ask yourself this question: where is my focus, what do I pour myself into the most?

Remember you hold your spouse's heart in your hands. Nobody else in the world has that power.

Ideally, a marriage should be a God covenant between two friends. Are you working at being each other's friend?

Allow the Word of God to set the standard for your relationship. There is a great deal of wisdom that can be applied to marriages in the Bible. Make the effort to find it and then apply it.

Realize that there are seasons to life. The love you share in your twenties is not the same love you have for each other after you have been married for thirty years. Dad and mom were married for sixty-seven years, and their love continued to grow every day. Daddy still saw that little gorgeous, sassy brunette when he looked at Mom. Mommy still saw the cocky muscle-bound preacher. They were still sweethearts with a history of love, trust, and living for each other behind them until death parted them. I want to ask you this: where do you want your relationship to be in ten, twenty, thirty, fifty years? Work now to build what you want things to be like then.

Romans 15:7 tells us to accept each other
just as Jesus Christ has accepted us.

Most marriages that end in divorce
begin to unravel because of petty little things
that are not dealt with, things like

— Why can't he pick up his socks, I'm not his maid.
— If she leaves the unfolded laundry on the bed one more time . . .
— I'm so sick and tired of being taken for granted.
— Doesn't she know the right way to hang toilet paper?
— If he really loved me he would know what I need.
— I am so sick and tired of having to compete with sports.

These all seem awfully petty, don't they?
Yet each one of these 'annoyances' can
become bricks in building a wall between you
and your spouse if you stuff them down
and do not deal with them.

Galatians 5:13 instructs us to serve each other in love. If we do this, our love for each other and the romance of our relationship will not grow cold, but blossom and grow greater every passing year.

Being one means you are not embarrassed or afraid to share your spiritual struggles, doubts, fears, convictions, your hopes and dreams (that deep, inner part of you that makes up who you are, the part you don't share with anyone else).

Cherish the uniqueness of your spouse as an individual and also the uniqueness of who the two of you are together. You are a precious gift to each other and to the body of Christ.

If there are problems in your relationship, take responsibility for your part in it. Ask the Lord to open your eyes to the things in you that need to go.

Work on the little irritations and challenges,
and the big ones will take care of themselves.
You prevent them from even showing up!

Marriage is held together by millions of fine gold and silk threads—threads like consideration, trust, kindness, respect, gentleness, praying together, not keeping score . . . etc.

Marriage can stretch you
to the breaking point on any given day,
and it is only by falling on your face before God
that you will become pliable enough not to break.

When was the last time you complimented your spouse in front of others? Don't be afraid to do so, but be sure the compliment is genuine.

A key to happiness is found in Phil. 4:11; I have learned to be content no matter what situation I find myself in. You will find no better place to apply this philosophy than in marriage.

Marriage is the relationship between a man and a woman where two completely separate people choose to become dependent on each other and committed to building the relationship on a covenant promise with God.

Proverbs 29:11 lets us know that a fool vents all his thoughts and feelings, not stopping to consider his/her words or the consequences they will bring, while a wise person holds them back! There are times when you have to just check your words and analyze your feelings rather than blurting out things which may cause harm and pain to the one you are speaking to. This could be your spouse, your children, someone you work with, etc. Consider your words!

Every marriage comes in its own form with its own challenges and blessings. However, the marriage covenant as shown to us throughout the Bible is constant and unchanging. Covenant relationship was established in the Garden of Eden. God does not go back on the principles that He establishes. Don't allow the standard of the day dictate the quality or standard of your relationship.

Marriage is so precious to the Lord that He likened it to the love relationship between the church (his bride) and Himself. Consider the extent he went to, to make that relationship possible. He gave everything for a relationship with us. Should we not make the effort as well to build a loving relationship between us and the one we promised to love and cherish? He gave absolutely everything.
What are you willing to give?

Consistently model a healthy respect and consideration for each other, make it a lifestyle; you never know who or when someone is watching. Let your life line up with what you say.

Never justify your poor behaviour or blame your spouse for it. Be mature enough to take responsibility for your own stuff.

Any relationship can survive a lot of storms if respect and appreciation for each other is firmly established before the storms hit.

Learn what 'romance' means to your spouse. We can guarantee you that it will be different from yours.

Don't put off until tomorrow what your relationship needs today. You don't want to look back with regret at things you should have done, but did not do.

Every couple needs to know that the other partner in the relationship speaks a 'different' language because each of us is a unique design, and no two people are alike. Our minds do not work the same, we are different genders, life experiences have shaped us differently, and we come from different backgrounds and family cultures. Women are relational in everything while men tend to categorize and put things in boxes. We all have something that makes us feel loved, and it is usually different than our spouse. Put a great deal of effort into learning each other's language and how the other 'ticks'. It will pay off in huge dividends.

Never be afraid to say, "I'm sorry."
When spoken in honesty, these words can bring healing and restoration quickly while building trust and security between you.

Your relationship with Jesus Christ is the most precious thing you can share as a couple. Treasure this gift as it is where the truest form of intimacy is to be found.

Any couple can grow into oneness if they are willing to work at it. Read books, go to weekend marriage retreats, seminars, etc.
Learn, learn, learn! Never stop putting in the effort to learn more. In most areas of our lives, we upgrade our education over the years. Should we not put the same effort into the most important relationship of our lives?

Look toward your future as a couple and keep watch for possible stumbling blocks or things that could be a threat to your relationship.

Faithfulness in marriage is not just physical, but being trustworthy, dependable and faithful in all areas of your life.

If your relationship is getting a little boring and predictable, plan a surprise for your sweetheart. Do something just for him/her that you would not do for you.
(Take him to a hockey or football game, bring her home some flowers or take her out to dinner. It does not have to be a huge thing, but just something that says you are thinking about them!) You get the idea!

When things are not going great, don't look at all the reasons why your marriage won't work. Look for reasons why it can and then work on them!

What you truly value, that is what you
will work for in your relationship.
What you set your heart and mind on,
what you consider valuable, will
determine how you will act towards each other.
It will build or tear down.

Today is the first day of the rest of your life,
so what do you want to do with the
rest of your life?
Take your first step toward what you want
your marriage to look like tomorrow.

Don't let go of the dreams you had in
your hearts when you got married.
Cherish them and make every effort
to make them come true.

Focus on what you have, not what you don't have. The grass really isn't greener on the other side of the fence.
Love what you have!

Tackle differences and misunderstandings quickly. The longer you leave them, the bigger they become and the harder they are to deal with.

There is a saying that goes something like this: "The person who is afraid of doing too much always ends up doing too little." Don't be afraid to pour everything into your marriage or you could eventually lose it.

God is the one who designed marriage, allow Him to be the center of yours.

Marriage has been likened to a pair of scissors. You cannot function as you were designed to without the other, often moving in opposite directions; but anyone who comes between you is in for some serious pain!

The marriage relationship between a man and a woman as God intended it to be is a lifetime of learning and growing into one entity while still being individuals. It is to be a permanent bond where many needs are satisfied.
These needs include friendship, need to love and be loved, sharing, companionship, sexual intimacy and satisfaction, family, trustworthy support, a place where you know your heart is safe and secure. It is a place where you are each other's top priority and where you can be the real you. There is nowhere else these needs can be met in one place.

There is no plan B in the will of God for marriage. Don't even let your mind wander there when things are not as good as you feel they should be.

Marriage will not be perfect, but if you give it top priority, it will flourish. It should be a place where neither spouse should have to hold back who they are or what they are feeling. It should be a place of mutual respect, submission, dedication, and determination.

Marriage is not the joining of two individual worlds as much as two worlds being left behind in order that a new world can be formed. A world, which has far greater potential than the two individual worlds alone.

God did not give you the job of 'fixing' your spouse, only He can do that. Pray blessing and abundance on them, and then get out of his way. Consider the fact that maybe there is something in you He wants to change and not your spouse after all! Allow Him to—for your sake and your spouse's.

Play together! Now guys, I know what you are thinking! No, that is not what we are talking about right here! This is 'shoulder to shoulder' stuff we are talking about. Find activities that you both enjoy like hiking, motorbikes, picnics, baseball, movies, checkers, or camping, anything that the two of you can do together outside the bedroom and enjoy. Make a point of getting out together and playing!

Take ownership of your behaviour; don't blame your spouse for making you mad or whatever emotion you are dealing with. Only you control your emotions, not your spouse.

Communication is to a relationship what the lifeblood is to the body. There will be no real life in a marriage without it. If you don't know how to communicate, find someone who can help you develop the skill.

One way to improve your marriage is to find things in you that you can improve. Take action, don't just think about these areas but do it—whether it is spiritual, mental, emotional, or physical. Just do it; like exercising, dieting, getting more education, taking music lessons, getting a haircut, climbing a mountain, whatever it is, just do it! You will be surprised at how much better you feel about yourself, which in turn affects everything else in your life.

Always keep in mind that the greatest battleground is in the mind. When negative things are battling in your mind, take authority over them in Jesus' name and choose to think positively about your spouse and situation. Pray for the one you promised to love and cherish. Ask the Lord to bless them!

In a disagreement, if you find yourself defending your faults or errors, it is usually a good sign that you aren't working that hard at changing things in you that need changing. Spend less time defending your position and more time working towards a solution that will benefit you as a couple.

There is absolutely nothing in life that can begin to compare to a good marriage.

You can accomplish with kindness and considerations far more than you will accomplish by force or nagging.

If your spouse's behavior is not mature and kind, it does not give you an excuse for poor behavior. Respond in an opposite spirit, and watch the storm that is brewing become calm.

If the atmosphere is not positive and loving in your home, what are you doing to change it?

Be you!
Shine and sparkle in your strengths and giftings and allow your spouse to do the same!

What you are inside where nobody can see it colours how you see life. If your marriage is good, it may have a great deal to do with the quality of your character! If your marriage is not good . . . look inward!

Let your kids see you showing affection. One of the sweetest memories of my childhood was seeing Daddy going up behind Mommy when she was cooking and kissing her neck and giving her a hug. Consider the imprint you are leaving on your family.

Men and women are created in the magnificent image of God himself. Keep this in mind as we look at a word that has, for years, been used to abuse and belittle many women in the body of Christ. A word that has left many women with an ugly taste in their mouth.

Submission: (our definition)
In the days of the knights, a king or prince of a country would go to another king who was at war battling a common enemy. He would submit himself (or willingly offer himself and all his resources) to that king. Together they would take on the common enemy and utilize each other's strengths in a united front to defeat their enemy. This did not make the king who offered his kingdom and resources less of a king, but a very valuable ally. The war king would confer with and come up with strategies with the ally king, utilizing his strengths to the greatest advantage. The war king would make the final decisions based on the input of the ally king. When the battle was won, both kings shared in the spoils of the battle.

Cont. on the next page . . .

Guys, the 'war king' would not browbeat or misuse or look down his nose at his ally king or his kingdom resources, but rejoice at the help and appreciate it, placing great value on it. The saying that 'behind every good man is a good woman' has a great deal of truth to it. Believe it! As you treat your wife as the most valuable and precious thing in your life, she will come alongside you, and you truly will become so much greater than you would be otherwise. Scripture says in Proverbs that a man who finds a wife finds a good thing (not because he has found himself slave labour, but a helpmate—one who brings out the best in him). Keep in mind what a good thing she really is, treat her accordingly, and she will not be able to do anything but respond in like manner.

Girls, in a marriage, when you submit to your husband's leadership you are saying to him, "I am coming alongside you with all I am. I'm bringing all my strengths and giftings, so that together we can be stronger and more effective, and we will both benefit far more than either of us would on our own." When you see yourself in this light, submission is a pretty awesome way to live.

Of all the things that occupy space in your mind throughout the day, be sure your spouse is one of them!

Don't measure the success of your marriage by how affluent you are. There are many 'poor' rich homes where love does not live and also many 'rich' poor homes where you will find love and acceptance in abundance.

Allow and encourage your spouse to be all that God created them to be, not who you think they should be.

When you face yourself honestly and admit your shortcomings and faults, it makes it much easier to allow your spouse their shortcomings and faults also.

Give of yourself without holding back, and you will find that you have little time left over to be critical of your spouse.

When in a fight, don't attack your spouse or their character, but attack the problem that is the cause of the conflict. Very often we use the word *you* when it should be *we.*

Reconciliation: going to someone to make things right for their benefit rather than just thinking about yourself and your benefit.

When you choose to forgive, it does not mean that what was done to you was right or that the person was right in what they did, but that you will not allow their behaviour to affect and control you.

Place yourself mentally, emotionally, and spiritually in a position to be accepting and learning from each other. Learn to recognize the Jesus in your spouse. Keep in mind that neither of you are perfect yet!

Do you have regrets, 'if onlys' in your relationship? How about letting them go and begin a brand-new page today. Turn your 'if onlys' into 'let's . . .'.

Choice—what a powerful gift! If you choose to do the right thing during those hard and difficult times, eventually your circumstances will change for the better.

When in a conflict situation, many of us like to blame our spouse for our reactions. Remember, you are the only one who can make you act a certain way. Your spouse cannot 'make' you feel or do anything. If you feel anger, it is not the other person who made you feel angry, you choose to feel angry and respond accordingly.

Have you ever gotten into a spat with your spouse and really blown it? Seek forgiveness, then grow from the experience. Let the situation be a stepping-stone in your journey to maturity rather than a stumbling block. Learn from your mistakes, and then keep an eye open for the next time the same situation or a similar one tries to raise its ugly head.

Consider this: right now is the most important minute of your marriage. What are you doing with it? Are you building or destroying?

If you love God and walk in the principles set out in the Bible, you always have a solid foundation to take a stand on and guideline for behaviour when your feelings don't line up with the commitment you made to each other on your wedding day.

This says it all!

sower of seed used by permission

This is such a perfect example of what many marriages look like and what they could accomplish with a little cooperation.

Marriage is about being free to be me while still being responsible and mature enough to do what is best for 'us'. When both of you see and understand this, it gives love a perfect environment to grow.

Just because your body is mature, it does not mean that you are! Take an inventory of yourself emotionally, mentally, and spiritually. Be honest with yourself and start working on one area today that needs it. This one honest step will impact your relationship for years to come!

Learn each other's 'love language'. What says "I love you" to your spouse? Not everyone needs the same thing to make them feel loved. It is very rare to find a husband and wife who need the same thing. Make the effort to find out what your spouse needs.

Before you get out of bed in the morning, look for some way that you can validate each other.

There are seven beliefs that we believe to be keys to a vibrant alive relationship:

First, have a vision for your marriage; see yourself in a happy, loving relationship. See your spouse as a vital part of you—treat him/her as well as you treat yourself.

Second, develop a healthy, godly self-image. How do you see yourself? Learn to see yourself as your Creator sees you and choose to be a good spouse.

Third, develop a healthy mind-set. Where does your mind naturally go, to the positive or to the negative? What is your attitude toward your spouse, and do you hear the tone of your voice when speaking to them?

Fourth, let go of the past and start fresh every day.

Fifth, find strength and joy in the hard times (James 1:2,3).

Sixth, live to be a giver. Keep in mind that what you sow you will reap in time. The more you pour into your marriage, the more will be there for you.

Seventh, make the choice to live joyfully. Even in tough circumstances, you can live above them because you choose not to live by emotion, but by the principles you find in the Word of God.

In Gen. 2:24, God spoke this commandment: leave your mother and father and cleave to your wife. This means that from the day you say "I do," your parents take second place in your life. One cause for disharmony in marriage is if the husband does not sever the ties with his mother and father and bond with his wife. Once you are married, there is no other person or thing in this entire world that should come before your wife. This works both ways; the wife needs to sever the apron strings as well. Because the relationship with our daughter is so strong, when she got married we strongly encouraged her and her new husband to move to another city for at least one year. This encouraged them to learn to lean on each other rather than to run to Mom and Dad for help. We have never regretted this move, and they haven't either.

Severing the ties does not mean you no longer value the opinions and advice of your parents, but rather you first go to each other when decisions have to be made; then if need be, you go together (both in agreement) to the parents.

A Topic of Great Interest!

Sex is the most beautiful gift God has given to married people yet so distorted and made cheap by the world's standard.

So why are the two genders so different? Why did He design women to warm up slowly like an oven and men switch on like a light bulb? Why does a man enjoy his wife wearing a cute little teddy? Why does she just want to wear flannel pyjamas that cover her from head to toe? Why is it all men think about is sex? Like always! Why is it that sex isn't that important to women?

SO MANY QUESTIONS!

We will deal with most of these questions in separate sections for guys and gals, but we will touch on a few here.

The wife gives authority over her body
to her husband, and the husband also gives
authority over his body to his wife.

Sex is God's idea. He stood back,
looked at his handiwork, and said,
"It is good, very good!" (Gen. 1:31).
We think he said it with a smile,
what do you think?

Sex is all about blessing your spouse,
not all about you!
God not only designed it for procreation,
but for recreation in the confines and
security of the covenant of marriage.
Take delight in each other!

Love with abandon! IT IS GOOD!
Remember that God said so.

The pleasure we can find in each other is very well described in the *Song of Solomon*. This is not X-rated material, but a love poem between a man and woman deeply in love. God chose to put it in the Bible so it's OK; go ahead, read it together, and see where it takes you!

It is said that a woman's body cycles about every twenty-eight days; a man cycles about once every forty-eight to seventy-two hours, and he thinks about sex about every four seconds.

Never withhold your bodies from each other using sex as a weapon or as a reward. Using sex this way is abusing something that should be precious between you, and it opens the doorway for all sorts of issues to enter a marriage that shouldn't be there.

First Corinthians 7:3-5 is very clear on how we are to relate sexually.
Do not deprive each other of sexual intimacy. The only exception to this rule would be the agreement of both husband and wife to refrain from sexual intimacy for a limited time so they can give themselves more completely to prayer. Afterward, they should come together again so that Satan won't be able to tempt them because of their lack of self-control.

When you and your spouse share in the pleasures of sex, we like to think of it this way, you are actually doing spiritual warfare. You are defeating the devil at one of his most common and low-down tricks. When things are good in the bedroom at home, the allure of sexual infidelity is drastically reduced. Your ability to look the other way when sin attempts to snare you is greatly strengthened when your sexual need is being met in a safe and loving environment with your spouse.

Sexual desire is a God-given desire. Your sexuality is a part of who you are by His design. Marriage provides the safe environment in which to satisfy this desire. Remember, He placed the desire there.

Our bodies are designed to fit together perfectly, to give and receive pleasure from each other. What an awesome design our God has created!

Sex is the only thing in this world that can create life. What an awesome responsibility God has given us—handle it with the awe and respect that it deserves.

God's heart is that sex between spouses would be motivated by the love and commitment they have for each other rather than by lust. Lust is self-seeking. Making love as God designed it to be is giving.

Never allow anger, resentment, or misunderstanding to interfere in your physical relationship. Always clear up misunderstandings so there is no coldness or walls between you.

Sex is the celebration of our commitment to each other. Matthew 19:4 tells us that when you leave your father and mother, be united to each other and become 'one flesh'.

Sexual intimacy is more than just a physical act. It is about exposing to your mate the very deepest and most intimate parts of who you are. Allow it to be your 'sweet place' with each other.

If you have trouble in the area of sex, don't be ashamed to seek help. Don't let sexual dysfunction destroy the sweetness in your relationship, which it can if not dealt with.

Always keep the marriage bed a place where you are safe and secure with each other. Don't allow Hollywood and the twisted ideas portrayed there to enter your secret domain. Remember, it is all about giving something to your sweetheart that nobody else can.

Don't let fear of not living up to the expectations of your spouse keep you from being bold and experimenting with each other.

Try to see things from your spouse's perspective. This will help you to give to your spouse what they need rather than giving them what you want them to give to you.

Flirt with each other! It makes him feel like Tarzan and makes her feel absolutely gorgeous and irresistible!

Try something new if your bedroom starts to become mundane and boring. Add a little variety, anything goes as long as both of you are comfortable with it.

Guys are visual, stimulated by sight, while women are relational. Guys, do things that seem foreign to you, and you will most likely be right on target or very close to what she needs. Girls, keep in mind that you can turn a guy upside down with just a certain movement or look. You have incredible power over your man. Use this for your husband only and have fun! Enjoy each other, and remember sex is God's idea, not Hollywood's. (Just thought I would remind you!)

Gain knowledge from godly sources. Some of the ideas we grew up with are wrong, so be open-minded and be willing to learn from each other.

Porn has absolutely no place in the bedroom of those who profess to love the Lord. Hebrews 13:4 tells us to keep our marriage bed pure and undefiled. There should only be the two of you there, completely absorbed in each other.

There are so many good books that have been written about sex that there is no reason to be ignorant about your love, how they tick, and what pleases them.

Among a few are
Sheet Music by Dr. Keven Leman,
Intimate and Unashamed by Dr. Scott Farhart,
Intimacy by Doug Weiss,
Intended for Pleasure by Jane Hansen,
The Act of Marriage by Tim and Bev LaHaye,
Sex According to God by Kay Arthur
and many more. Go to your Christian bookstore and pick up a couple then enjoy!

Proverbs 14:1

Every wise woman builds her house, but the foolish pulls it down with her hands

To be the precious gift to your man that God desires you to be you need to learn. Find an older woman whose life you admire and ask her to mentor and teach you. Allow her to inspire you and encourage you in your role as wife and mother, but also in the spiritual area of life as well.

Spend time searching the Word of God for wisdom on being a good spouse. As you read, you will find the Bible is a book that is full of principles you can apply to every day living. Then go out and be a doer of the word and not just a hearer of it.

Always keep in mind that you're the heart of the home. The woman usually sets the general tone and atmosphere in her home.

Sex is your love gift to your husband; a gift that you want reserved for you alone! To a man it says, "I love you." Women may not understand the way a man thinks or why he thinks he needs sex so often, but it really doesn't matter if we understand, just know that this is how God made him and bless him with your body.

Encourage your hubby! Don't lecture or criticize him as this does just the opposite to what you want.

Consider yourself to be your man's very best present and go out of your way to make yourself beautiful and seductive for him (him alone!).

Men like to come across as tough, capable, able to handle the world with one hand tied behind their back. Do you realize that only you can build his manliness and confidence to the level where he really can face the world and win? You can also tear that confidence down and destroy it with careless, unkind words and a critical attitude.

Don't compete with your husband. Use your personality and your strengths to compliment!

Your man needs to know he makes you happy. Let him see and enjoy your heartfelt smile.

To all outward appearances, your man may look to be confident, secure, and full of self-assurance, but under the disguise is still the little boy who needs somebody who believes in him and will defend him regardless of circumstances.

Just as women need to feel secure in their place in their man's life, so he needs to feel secure in the fact that you believe in him and respect him.

Of all the needs your man has, sex is his greatest physical need, and respect from you is his greatest emotional need.

Of all the things your man would love to see you wear to bed—a positive attitude is probably the best of all!

If you have had sexual experiences in your past that were not according to the way God planned, whether your fault or not, face the pain and deal with it. Get professional help if you need it. Find out what God says about who you are in Jesus (that beautiful creature that Psalms 139 talks about) then, move on!

When your hubby brings you a gift
or flowers or helps you around the house or
with the kids, he is telling you several things
all at one time:
He is thinking about you (he'd like sex).
He appreciates you (he'd like sex).
He approves of you and values you (he'd like sex).
He feels safe and secure in you (he'd like sex).
He wants to be close to you (he'd like sex).
Do I need to say more?

A woman's body is the most fascinating thing in the world to a man. Be pleased that your man appreciates your packaging. Do everything you can to be beautiful for him. He will always appreciate a beautiful woman and will always be surrounded by them; keep in mind however, it is you he comes home to at the end of the day.
(Don't meet him with curlers in your hair!)

Are there times when you resent the fact that God made you a woman? God does not make mistakes. Psalms 139 tells us that He formed your innermost parts (your femininity as well as your soul) and knit you together in the womb of your mother. You are wonderfully made; and deep down inside, when you consider how you are made, you know it is true. You were not hidden from God when you were being formed, but He was there putting you together, embroidering you with various glorious colours. Have you really looked at an intricate embroidery or tapestry? The workmanship is marvellous and breathtaking! You are even more breathtaking! Not only did He take the time to design and assemble you perfectly, but then He wrote down in His book all the days He had planned for you. These plans include being a sexual being. Stop and consider your sexuality and remember that God stood back and declared it good! Enjoy the beauty and intimacy with your husband God created you for.

One way to help your man feel like a man is to embrace who the Lord made you to be as a woman. It is okay to be soft and gentle as God designed a woman to be, and it is all right to allow your man to be the strong protector, which is part of his God-given nature. Men love to be needed!
Sometimes that old 'knight in shining armour rescuing his damsel in distress' mentality is just what he needs to feel masculine and good about himself. Allow him to be the man!

Sex is one of the greatest ways that a man feels connected and close to his wife.

Build him up with your words!
Proverbs speaks of a wise woman building her home while a foolish one tears it down.
Words are a very effective tool in this process either for good or for destruction.
Use your words wisely!

You can be a sensuous being and be spiritual at the same time; remember that God designed you sensuous. (Not sensual as the world dictates: sleazy and cheap but delighting in and enjoying the senses —what you are as a whole woman)

There is absolutely nothing wrong with admiring your man's muscles or whatever it was that attracted you to him in the first place.
Let him know you find him sexy and masculine and you will have him eating out of your hand!
This is not to manipulate, but to build up!
Nothing can build up your man like a well-placed word of admiration from his wife.

Go out and buy that cute little 'teddy' or negligee!
Be bold and daring for him, don't let your sex life become mundane and boring.
Push yourself out of your comfort zone and throw him for a loop once in a while.
He will love it! We guarantee it!

Make your man a hero to your kids. When we were little, Mom would station one of us at the front window to watch for Daddy when it was time for him to come home. When we saw him, we gave the signal (usually a war whoop), and we all rushed to the door to wait for him. As soon as he opened the door, we jumped on him. We got our hugs and kisses then Daddy would pat us and say, "Okay, it's Mommy's turn now!" We loved to see Dad giving Mommy her hugs and kisses, it made us feel very secure. This is a tradition I carried into our home for those years when the children were young, and I remained at home with them. Not every wife is fortunate enough to stay home to raise the children, but there are many ways you can enforce the value of Dad with your kids. Teach them how to do 'special' things for Dad for no other reason than just because they and their mom love him. Make Dad a hero to your kids! It reinforces your love for him as it builds love and admiration for him in your kids. What a precious gift to give not only your kids, but their dad too.

Get in shape! Sex is far better for you when your weight is where it should be. When you feel good about your body, it directly affects how you feel about sex.

Your man will really love it if once in a while you take the initiative in loving rather than him always having to be the aggressor. Allow yourself to delight in his body and the pleasure you can give him.

Make occasions to laugh together.
Being an adult with responsibility does not mean that you can't do things that are fun.
Enjoy laughter.

For years, the church has taught men that they are to love their wives as Christ loved the church. The flip side—your side—is to honour and respect your man. He needs that more than you will ever know!

If he has to go out of town for a trip, why not write him little notes of encouragement and 'promise' and tuck them in his socks! He will do everything in his power to get home as quickly as possible!
If he takes a lunch, occasionally tuck a 'sweet note' in with his sandwiches (a little promise for tonight that will curl his toes!).
Not only is this fun, but it keeps up the excitement and romance in a relationship.

A bit of advice my mom gave me when I was first married: "Keep him happy at home and he will never wander." I knew she spoke of the physical part of marriage but also a great deal more than that. There is nothing like a happy and peaceful home to give a man a reason to look forward to the end of the day.
Is your home a place he wants to come home to?

Proverbs 18:22 tells us that when a man finds a wife he finds a good thing.
When struggling with womanhood, remember
YOU ARE A GOOD THING!

GUYS

This section is just for you!

Ephesians 5:28
In the same way, husbands ought to love their wives as they love their own bodies. For a man is actually loving himself when he loves his wife.

Admit you need your wife—to her face! Look her in the eyes and tell her you need her like you need the air you breathe, then act that way! These words and actions of affirmation and value bring out a beauty in your sweetheart that nothing else can!

Good sex starts at supper, great sex starts when you get home from work, and incredible sex starts at breakfast and goes all day long—let me explain! Romance all day. A look (you know, the kind you used to give her when you picked her up for a date and she was stunning like—knock your socks off!). Help pick up after the kids, flowers once in a while, help clean off the supper table, open her door for her, call in the middle of the day to touch base and let her know she is on your mind . . . etc. You don't need to do this constantly, but be real with it. Make appreciating her a lifestyle.

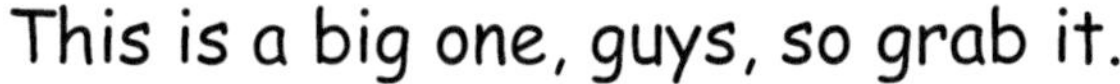

This is a big one, guys, so grab it.

A man can meet a deep need in his wife just by listening to her when she needs to talk. You may feel what she has to say is of no consequence to you; however, she needs to express her feelings, it makes her feel connected to you.
Validate her feelings even if you feel they are unreasonable or illogical. This does not mean you have to agree!
Remember, men and women's minds run on different tracks but compliment each other.
Just listen, don't argue, give solutions, offer to 'fix it', or tell her that what she feels is silly and makes no sense or that her thinking is wrong.
Her feelings are still her feelings.
Allow her to share her heart with you.
This truly says, "I love you" in the language a woman understands.

If you have an incredible wife, chances are you are doing something very right. If you have a miserable, crabby wife, look in the mirror for the reason then take some steps to turn things around.

When you bring home a little token of love like flowers or a gift (it does not have to be a big thing), or spend time with her doing something that she likes to do, she is hearing you say several things: approval, appreciation, affection, she is on your mind . . . etc. This makes her heart feel secure and safe in your care, chances are she might be a lot more inclined to want sex too!

God designed women to be responders. Give her something good and positive to respond to and your home will be the castle you always dreamed it would be.

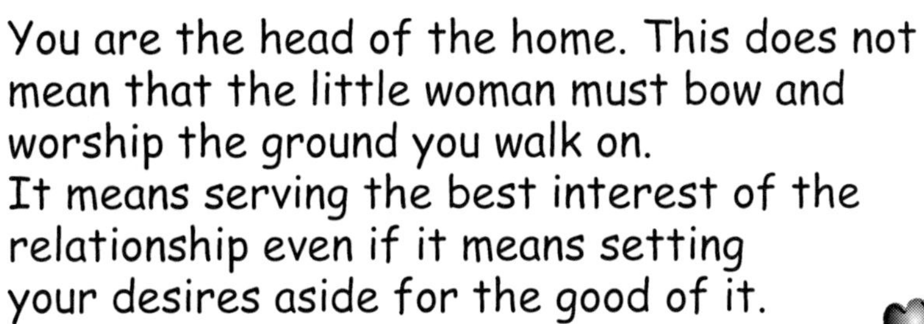

You are the head of the home. This does not mean that the little woman must bow and worship the ground you walk on.
It means serving the best interest of the relationship even if it means setting your desires aside for the good of it.

If your wife is sharing her heart with you (which are her feelings) and she feels you are not really listening, it could hurt and even wound her. This may make no sense to you, but look at her, ask questions, make positive comments. Stick with her—hear her heart.

Your wife needs to feel cherished, and small expressions mean far more to her than a man can possibly understand.
Cherished in the dictionary is this—adored, listened to, complimented, feel protected, cared for, touched often (nonsexually), accepted.
Wow, it will take a bit of work guys, but it will be well worth the effort.

Let your wife know how much you appreciate all those mundane things she does around the home every day (you know, like picking up your dirty socks, feeding you, etc.) all those things that make your home a nice place to come home to.

Do something for her that she knows you really don't enjoy doing. (Not expecting anything; women see right through that!) Just do it to let her know how you love and appreciate her.

Don't demand! Ask.

Touch her often (no, don't grope, I said touch!). Find out the ways she enjoys being touched, whether a touch on her shoulder as you walk by, a quick kiss on the cheek, a squeeze of the hand. Every woman is different, so put in the effort to find out what pleases yours.

In 1 Peter chapter 3, it tells men to live in understanding with their wives or their prayers will not be heard by their Heavenly Father. This can be a tough one because it means you have to make every effort to learn to understand how a woman feels and thinks! I wish you the best—women are complicated creatures! I have been at it for over thirty-five years and still don't have mine figured out, but it sure is fun trying! Life will never be dull for you.

If your wife is a stay-at-home mom, never take that luxury for granted. It is a fortunate family that has a mom at home to raise and guide the children. Make sure you let her know that you appreciate her caring for your home and your most valuable treasure—your kids.

Consider the cost of hiring someone to come in and care for your home—that is measurable. There is, however, no way to measure the value of moulding and nurturing a human life.

Sex is extremely important to a man, and often men wonder why their wives are not as eager to make love as they are. Guys, one way to ensure that your girl is more eager than she may be otherwise is to make every effort to please her and bring her to fulfillment before you allow yourself the same pleasure. Don't be embarrassed or too proud to ask her what she enjoys and allow her the freedom to let you know what she does not enjoy. Keep the lines of communication open and loving, free of any feelings of inadequacy and condemnation. Keep in mind that when a woman gives herself to her husband she is opening herself up totally and becoming extremely vulnerable to you. Her vulnerability is the most precious gift she will ever give you.
Handle it with gentleness and care.

Sex should be good, clean fun! She will be more receptive to you if you smell and feel fresh and clean. We have made it a habit of having a shower every night before bed. Nothing feels quiet as good as clean skin on skin.

Practice 'loving' habits daily. Remember how you treated her when you were courting? If things have dried up, bring them back to life by working on making her feel as wanted and loved as when you were trying to win her heart.

Because husbands are to be the head of the home, it means you are the one who is responsible for the provision for the family, not her. Even if she takes care of the books or works outside the home and brings in a share of the money, it is still your responsibility before God to make sure there is provision for your family's needs.

Guard your heart and mind against porn. It can destroy not only you, but your wife as well. Keep in mind God's design for sex—a gift to be shared between two people who are committed to each other in the boundaries of marriage.

If your marriage is in turmoil, choose to do the right thing. Rise up and take responsibility for the relationship as the head of the family. Do the right thing even if it isn't comfortable or what you want to do. Fight for your family, not with them. Cover them with your protection. Be the hero to your wife and kids that they need you to be.

As you cherish your wife and protect her heart, you will find her more responsive and respectful of you.

Teach your children how to live a godly life by the way you live, not just by telling them how to live. Words really mean very little unless they are backed up by your life in attitudes and actions.

There is a saying that goes something like this:
children spell love—TIME. Guys, it isn't just
children, but wives as well. Make time for her.
Set aside special time for family every
day even if it means missing your sports on TV.
Time moves so fast, and one day
you will look back over your
life and wonder where it all went.
Don't miss the precious gift that God
has given you in your wife and children.
Make them your priority in life.
Enjoy your 'now'.

There is an old saying that goes like this:
life is fragile handle with prayer.
Cover the ones you love every day with prayer;
it is the most powerful tool
that God has given you.

Above all else, be kind!

There are a great number of books on the market that are designed to help you grow in understanding and Godly relationship principles. Listed are just a few of our favorites.

Love & Respect - Emmerson Eggerichs
Sheet Music - Kevin Leman
The DNA of Relationships - Gary Smalley
Intimacy - Douglas Weiss
Straight Talk - James Dobson
The Secret of Loving -- Josh McDowell
The Act of Marriage - Tim & Bev LaHaye
The Five Love Languages - Gary Chapman
Intimate and Unashamed - Scott Farhart
Boundaries in Marriage - Cloud & Townsend
Love is a Decision - Gary Smalley & John Trent
Men are like Waffles Women are like Spaghetti - Bill & Pam Farrel
Communication the Key to Marriage - H Norman Wright
Sex According to God - Kay Arthur
Every man's battle - Stephen Arterburn, Fred Stoerker
Every heart restored - Stephen Arterburn, Fred & Brenda Stoeker
Every woman's battle - Shannon Ethridge
Men: Some Assembly Required - Chuck Snyder
Wild At Heart (Understanding a Man's Soul) - Elderidge

There are many more excellent books, so invest in your marriage and get an education from those who have been there and can help you.

Contact information

Heartcare
moral based relationship coaching

Heart Care Ministries
Box 5183
Drayton Valley AB
Canada
T7A 1R4
email: thomtfb@telus.net
or link at
Drayton Valley Word of Life Centre
780 621 0277
website: dvwordoflife.com

If this book has been a help and encouragement to you, we would love to hear from you.

CPSIA information can be obtained at www.ICGtesting.com
Printed in the USA
LVOW080927290912

300782LV00002B/1/P